ORCHIDS

GROWING ORCHIDS MADE EASY AND PLEASANT

The Most Common Errors In The Cultivation Of Orchids

Let Your Orchids Grow For Many Years

D1463096

MIRANDA ROSS

TABLE OF CONTENTS

3

INTRODUCTION

The world over, orchids have held a fascination with their exotic appearance and their vibrant colors. The earliest written or pictorial evidence of orchids is in Chinese and Japanese art & literature as long ago as circa 700BC. The history of orchid discovery and the subsequent increasing interest in these plants proves that they have a strong lure for anyone who sees them. Unlike earlier days when orchids were very expensive and accessible only to a few, today they have become plants that everyone can enjoy and afford.

The book aims to familiarize you with different aspects of the orchid plant before getting started. The aim of this endeavor is to help beginners realize that growing orchids is like having a pet. If you pay attention to them they will repay you with lovely blooms. If you wish to grow this spectacular plant in your garden, but thought that it was too difficult, then this book will help you to get started.

Even if you have failed to bloom orchids in the past, there are several tips and techniques to help you keep your orchids blooming, no matter your environment or experience, budget and location. The book demystifies the growing process and reveals professional secrets for blooming, repotting and pests. Perfect for beginners as well as orchid experts looking for new tricks, you will discover which orchids are the easiest to grow, and then learn the steps you need to take to keep your orchid alive, healthy and blooming.

Happy Growing!!!

DISCLAIMER: The purpose of this book is to provide information only. The information, though believed to be entirely accurate, is NOT a substitution for medical, psychological or professional advice, diagnosis or treatment. The author recommends that you seek the advice of your physician or other qualified health care provider to present them with questions you may have regarding any medical condition. Advice from your trusted, professional medical advisor should always supersede information presented in this book.

KNOW YOUR ORCHIDS

Orchids are the most spectacular, distinctive and diverse type of flowers. Certainly, there is no flower as popular and desired as them. The popularity of the orchid flower can be contributed to a number of factors which include their wonderful fragrance, their delicate beauty and their colorful blooms. The exotic flowers are now grown in a wide range of colors and people like to associate them with very special occasions.

With their subtle beauty and historical rarity, orchids carry an unrivaled sense of refinement. They are the largest family of plants with over 20,000 known species. It is said that you could acquire a different orchid every day for eighty years and still not be able to grow all of them.

HISTORY OF ORCHIDS

America, Canada and Eurasia are known to be the homeland for orchids but today they are found in almost all parts of the world except for the arid zones. In Europe avid interest in orchids can be traced back to Greek and Roman times. Like many ancient civilizations, the Greeks focused on the resources of the natural world. The tubers and roots of most European terrestrial orchids were valued for various medicinal purposes. They studied the many uses of the orchid flowers and believed that their different shapes revealed the many benefits of the plant.

The word orchid is derived from the Greek "orchis" meaning testes referring to the tubers found in pairs in some species. In the New World, orchids were used by the inhabitants long before the arrival of Europeans. The Aztecs grew this vine-like orchid which they called Tlilxochitl, for the seed capsules, which were ground and mixed with the brown seeds of the cacao plant to produce a bitter drink that is the basis of the chocolate.

It is not vital to trace the history of Orchid cultivation since its start, a century and a half ago. The earlier references were few and infrequent, but they attracted as much attention as orchids in our gardens do today. It may be said of Orchids that few other plants have over the years consistently sustained the interest of cultivators. This is partly because very few plants have flowers that exhibit such diversity, size and dazzling display of colors. Long prized by collectors and cultivators, orchids are commonly believed to be difficult to grow and maintain. In fact, many varieties are as easily grown as any other plant with a little bit of care and dedication.

DIFFERENT VARIETIES OF ORCHIDS

There are as many as 20,000 species with the family Orchidae, that bear some of Earth's most flamboyant flowers. Several thousand more varieties may await discovery. However, there are more than a hundred thousand hybrid species grown for both commercial and decorative purposes the world over. Orchids are the most adaptable flower species and found in almost all climates. They come in myriad colors and shapes. They have three sepals, three petals and labella. The third petal is lip shaped to attract insects for pollination. Some of them take on the shape of bees and moths while some others have distinct smells to attract insects for cross-pollination.

Many of the orchids are epiphytes and they grow on trees with their roots hanging to the tree's bark. The roots have an outer whitish layer called velamen that absorbs moisture from the air helping them to stay attached to the tree bark. Lithophytes are orchids that grow on rocks. Terrestrial orchids are those which grow on the ground. Temperate orchids are typically terrestrial, while tropical orchids usually are epiphytic.

Orchids exhibit mainly two types of growth patterns: Monopodial and Sympodial. Orchids that grow vertically have one main stem with leaves growing on either side. The tip where growth takes place is at the end of the stem with flower stems emerging from between the leaves in the main stem.

Sympodial orchids possess a horizontal stem through many vertical extensions emerge. Pseudobulbs are thickened stems found at the base of new bud making it easier for the orchid to propagate. Orchids can be fragrant. Some smell nice like citrusy or vanilla and here can be some nasty ones also. There are lots of miniature orchids that stay small like Pleurothallids, Ascocentrums, Bulbophyllums. They may be small, but equally beautiful.

Orchids are primarily two types; one that grows on the ground like Cattleya and second are those that grow on trees like Cymbidium. Some species grow on waste matter, but are not beautiful. They care be further classified under two main sub-types depending on the method of propagation. Some orchids multiply by lateral growth like the Cattleya and some by an atypical multiplication like in the Vanda plant. Orchid plants need optimum temperature and light to grow well with proper watering and humidity to flower. The common ones will be described.

BUYING ORCHIDS
WHAT TO LOOK FOR

Cymbidium

Buying orchids seems very simple.

The beginner has no idea what to look for when buying the first orchid or even the next one. The most common mistake is that we look at flowers and bewildered by the charm of these flowers we pay no attention to other things. It is normal that we want to pick the prettiest one with many flowers and buds.

In order to avoid this, however, you must have some information to avoid disappointment, and grown a new orchid does not entail costs of treatment or pest management.

If the orchid is only intended to decorate the interior for a short time, it is enough that plant looks nice. If we are going to grow it over the next few years we should carefully check under what conditions the plant lives in its natural environment and will we be able to provide the right conditions in our home. If we are unable to provide similar conditions, climate or lighting, better not to buy such an orchid. Because we condemn immediately the possible failure.

For example, Cambria orchids. Under this trade name is a huge group of hybrids with very different requirements so orchid producers assume that it will be a one-off product. Why is that? Conditions for growing should be very close to what their parents need. This is difficult to achieve. Such orchids will bloom once or twice, using the stocks accumulated in the production process and then, unfortunately, will not be easy to get orchids to re-bloom if we do not provide them with the necessary conditions.

LOOK AT THE SUBSTRATE IN WHICH THE ORCHID GROWS

If it is a medium containing large amounts of moss, algae this indicates that the plant grew in a high humidity and high temperature greenhouse. We are not able to provide such conditions for our orchids on the windowsill. Also changing the substrate and cultivation in a different substrate and air humidity are already exposing our orchid to a stressful start.

The residue from the early production period is another problem. Some orchids, as a seedling plant, grew in a rolled up moss in a little pot, in high humidity and in temperature suitable for such cultivation. Such moss is hidden deep between the roots. Unfortunately we do not see this in shop. Such post-production "rolled up" moss covered by soil in a new pot is a big threat to orchid's health. If the orchid is on the windowsill later, due to the cold surface, such coiled moss will be cold constantly. This will cause root rot and will quickly destroy the plant. Be aware that after the purchase you will have to pick up this moss.

In the markets often orchids are over watering and such long-term hydration is usually the reason of over-hydration of orchids and it causes them to rot.

The substrate in the pot should not be compact or too fibrous. It cannot be very soaked because it indicates its condition that the substrate is very spread. Medium for orchids with thick roots like Phalaenopsis, should be thick granulated, and the substrate for Miltonia or Oncidium for example should consist of finer pieces. the production substrates rarely meet the needs of home cultivation, because they are adapted to the needs of growing under other conditions. Therefore, almost every plant has to be repotted in a short time from purchase. When transplanting orchids, a suitable substrate for the species in terms of granulation and composition must be used.

INSPECT THE ROOTS

Say no to a plant that has excessive water and brown rotting roots.

Roots are the most important organ of orchid plants. Healthy roots mean healthy orchid. Orchid roots rapidly collect water and perform photosynthesis.

A healthy orchid's roots are firm and hard. They become silver or light green when dry and dark green when wet. The roots must be healthy, white with green ends.

Aerial roots (that grow or loop above the surface) should be firm, they may be dry but this is not dangerous.

The plant stops using old roots and they dry up. I do not even remove the old roots, because they often release branches and continue to function.

Dead roots are tan and shriveled when wet. An orchid with a small amount of healthy roots will be more difficult to cultivate. There is a risk that such orchid will lose the rest of the roots faster, especially during flowering. If the orchid has most of the empty or dark roots over its entire length, do not buy such a plant.

How to check the root condition when the flowerpot is not transparent? An orchid with sick or damaged roots "flies" loosely (or falls out of the pot) and after that you can roughly know that the root condition is probably poor.

It is important to check the condition of the roots after the purchase, because an orchid reacts quite late to the absence of healthy roots.

LOOK AT THE LEAVES

Check to see that the leaves and pseudobulbs are spongy and not dry.

Pay attention to the appearance of green parts. There are so many varieties among orchids, so leaves will not look the same. Some have thin leaves, while others have flat and thick leaves. Phalaenopsis is a non-resting orchid and should always have a firm leaves of impeccable looks.

Leaves should be firm, hard, irrigated without any signs of mechanical damage. Every injury is a place where they can easily infect fungi, bacteria and viruses. Check the plant's leaves for spotting, as they must be a healthy light green and not dark green. Avoid spotted plants as it indicates exposure to extreme temperatures that is harmful to the plant.

Flaky leaves can be found in orchids of some species, where flowering occurs after a period of rest. This is true for them - flowering during the non-vegetative period. However, the drying of leaf tips should not be a threat. These tips can be trimmed. Such changes on thin leaves are caused by too low air humidity in relation to the needs of the orchid. Oncidium sometimes has yellowish leaves. This is the result of excessive sun exposure. Such appearance does not indicate the poor condition of the plant. Young growth in good light will have the correct color of the leaves. It is also not disturbing that the oldest leaf will turn yellow. Phalaenopsis can lose in one year the 2 oldest leaves. The plant takes from these leaves the ingredients contained in them and uses them to nourish the young leaf or flowering flower. In this way the orchid preserves almost the same number of leaves in subsequent years.

If an orchid loses a young leaf, we have a hint that something bad is happening with the root system or there was a flooding near the leaf.

There are also Phalaenopsis, which have a flowering stem growing in place from which should grow a new leaf (from the cone of growth). Such orchid will not grow properly, blooms but no produces new leaves. It may give birth to a baby at the base, but the flowering of this young orchid is moving in time, and the mother plant usually disappears. Such orchids are the result of human manipulation in the early stages of plant development.

SIZE AND QUANTITY OF FLOWERS

Try to buy an orchid with some blooms and a few buds so that the flowers can last for a longtime.

We mostly choose orchids that have beautiful flowers already opened. This is the moment when we admire the color of flowers and forget about a few important things. It is good to keep in mind that orchids do not bloom long. Flowering usually lasts only a few months, may be shorter depending on the growing conditions. So buying an full bloom orchid make sure the plant does not lose any flower yet. Other blooms might wilt faster than you expect it. Avoid plants with stale looking flowers since the flowers will soon fall off. For this reason, it is best to buy a plant with the biggest number of unopened blooms.

It is best to buy flowering plants, and even multi-flow, because not all orchids increase the number of shoots in the next year. The size of the flowers will be similar to those of the purchase, because there are orchids of great flowers, small and tiny. Their size will not change with the next flowering.

The stem length is also important. The longer the stem the more flowers and branches it can produce. It also indicates the condition of the plant and its ability to bloom again. An orchid with magnificent long shoots is a unique specimen. With the right cultivation such orchid will be able to produce the same long stems as at the time of purchase.

Blue orchids such as Phalaenopsis and Dendrobium appear in shops. These are dyed plants. They are sold at a much higher price, and their color is not lasting. After some time orchid removes this dye and releases white flowers. You have to be aware that this is an action directed towards a greater profit for the producer (Phalaenopsis by nature never have blue flowers).

You should not buy orchids with streaks on the leaves, with distorted flowers, with discoloration on the flowers, which symptoms may indicate some illness changes.

ORCHIDS ON SALE

Buying cut-priced orchids is already a risk included in the purchase. You need to count on extra costs and time that you will have to sacrifice for healing the plant. The cost of basic treatment usually exceeds the price of a healthy orchid. In addition, the next flowering can take two to three years (e.g. Phalaenopsis), so it is important to consider such a purchase.

If an orchid has any symptoms of root disease or any green part, there is always an additional risk that the disease will be difficult or impossible to control and will migrate to other plants. Pests that damage orchids "open the gates" to the viruses, fungus, bacteria.

You should choose orchids without symptoms and suspicion of pests. Orchids might be dry, but they must have an impeccable root system.

Buying any orchid at a normal price or discounted, it is worth also looking at neighboring plants - often the whole group is infected with disease or has pests, then the risk increases very much that something like this may occur to the plant chosen by us.

GROW YOUR ORCHIDS

CHOOSING THE RIGHT VARIETY TO GROW

Cymbidium Frida

Growing orchids is addictive! Once you know how to grow orchids, they'll thrive for you. They will have more blooms each year. Growing orchids is simple and easy. If you imitate

24

a plant's natural habitat, it will flourish. There are several types of orchids so there is almost certainly an orchid that likes the conditions you can provide. The most commonly available orchids, such as the Moth Orchid or Phalaenopsis, are so popular because they grow well in homes.

Regardless of the many types of orchids you choose to grow, a few tricks and tips will help you keep them flowering. Growing orchids for beginners mostly involves learning a few basics. Once you have perfected that you will have a lovely bloom of these exotic flowers. Initially, when you cultivate orchids at your home choose Odontoglossums, Cymbidiums and Phalaenopsis. These three varieties are among the easiest to grow. Odontoglossums flower every nine months for up to four weeks and come in multiple colors. You can grow them inside the house and must be kept in a cool area away from the sun. They need to be repotted only once every two or three years. They may flower twice a year under optimum conditions. The plant bears small flowers in a bunch that look stunning.

Another popular orchid that is ideal for beginners is Phalaenopsis. The orchid flowers several times a year from a single stem and can last for several weeks. This plant grows well in a warm environment and can withstand dryness. They come in a wide array of colors and designs.

Phalaenopsis requires less water and low light. Cymbidium orchids bloom every winter for six to eight weeks. They need regular watering but not as much sun. They come in myriad colors and can grow to a huge size. These orchids thrive in a cool environment, so keep them in the sun only for a few hours in summer.

Other suitable varieties for the home growers include Bulbophyllum, Dendrochilum, Vanda, Dendrobium, Epidendrum, and Aerangis. These plant types grow well under indirect light and do not need extra care.

Oncidium plants come in a profusion of colors and are robust so they can adjust to the environment at home. The. Dendrobium and its hybrid varieties bloom in to a bunch of white flower lasting for several days. Vandas are epiphytes that grow on trees and so most people grow them outdoors. They come in a variety of colors but grow slowly. Another easy to grow orchid is the Epidendrum. It has a reed like appearance and produces several small flowers. Paphiopedilums grow well under fluorescent tubes and produce exquisite flowers shaped like a lady's slippers.

CHOICE OF LOCATION

Once you take the proper care, it is quite easy to cultivate orchids. Orchids are excellent indoor plants and some are easy to grow in a windowsill while some others require special conditions. According to available conditions at home you can choose the type that can help you maintain an orchid garden at home with blooms all year. They bloom the best between December and April.

Certain environmental factors are necessary for growing orchids in the natural environment as orchids do not grow directly in soil. They cling to trees with the help of their thick roots. This way, they absorb whatever water and air is available. Hence, they have natural adaptation abilities to survive without water for long because they store sufficient supply in their thick stems, leaves, and roots. It is vital to create a similar atmosphere at home.

When buying an orchid plant, examine the leaves and roots of the plant. Buy them from a reliable orchid grower or nursery. This ensures a good quality plant and the experts can help you with tips on nurturing and maintaining your orchid. Talk to the orchid grower about the type of orchid you would like to grow and describe your home environment. This is necessary because orchids need proper light, humidity and temperature for optimum growth.

Before buying the orchid, ensure that it sits firmly in the potting material and is insect free. Always ask the seller details about the amount of light & water required and the right temperature for the orchid plant you purchase. Do not compromise on the quality of the plant as a good plant can last for years with good care.

TAKING THE APPROPRIATE STEPS

The next step is to choose the right variety keeping in mind the conditions you can provide for the plant to thrive. Once you buy an orchid, transfer it to a proper container with the right potting mixture and take care not to break the roots. Keep the orchid plant in a well-lit area with proper air circulation. For optimum growth, water only when required and add fertilizer once a fortnight.

Do not expose them to the strong afternoon sun at any time as excessive sunlight can cause leaf spotting and discoloration. Accordingly, place the plants in a sunny or shaded area.

PROTECT YOUR ORCHIDS

Orchids appear delightfully exquisite and can attract anybody towards them. Orchids are excellent indoor plants, while some are easy to grow in a windowsill, some require special conditions Orchids bloom easily in the home environment and do not require extensive facilities. Primarily there are three main requirements for growing orchid home: proper light, temperature, and humidity. Few of the orchid species have specific requirements of light and temperature. Therefore, select the species that can adapt to the prevalent environment at your home.

KEY FACTORS FOR ORCHID BLOOMS

LIGHT

Orchids require good sunlight for around six hours a day. Optimum light increases the flowering potential of orchids. Lack of sufficient light may not hinder growth but is likely to affect its blooming capacity. The leaf color of orchids indicates if available light is optimum, dark green leaves indicate lack of sufficient light while light green with tinges of yellow indicates requisite light.

Excess light can bleach orchid leaves and lead to a slow death of your orchid plant. Otherwise, you can move the pots away from sunlight, if in excess. You can also provide artificial light by placing four fluorescent tubes of four feet each at a distance of six inches from one another.

The special grow lights although expensive provide good results. The directions of the windows in the house also play a significant role, southern- and eastern-facing windows work best for orchids, whereas western windows can be too hot in the afternoon and northern ones are usually too dark. Move plants away from or toward the window to manipulate the amount of light. Insufficient Light is the primary reason orchids do not bloom again.

TEMPERATURE

One of the most important matters in Orchid cultivation is temperature control. Orchids are usually classified as warm growing, intermediate and cool growing depending on their temperature needs. Many varieties can tolerate exposure to warmer or cooler temperatures without suffering much damage. Most varieties of orchids like the same temperatures and hate air conditioning. It is important to see that lower temperatures are maintained at night than in the day. You need to ensure that the temperature at home drops by at least 10 degrees at night, especially in autumn and winter. When orchids initiate buds, this will certainly help induce the orchids to set flower buds more readily. If this can be achieved, then this little trick can mean the difference between an orchid plant that merely lives, and one that thrives with wonderful blooms.

The temperature groupings refer to the lowest temperature the orchid prefers during winter nights. Warm-growing orchids, such as Phalaenopsis, are likely to complain if temperatures drop much below 60 °F/around 16 °C. Intermediate growers, such as Cattleyas, prefer winter nights around 55 °F/ around 13 °C. Cool-growing orchids, including Cymbidiums and Odontoglossums, are accustomed to winter nights of 50 °F/ 10 °C. As a rule, most orchids perform poorly when exposed to temperatures above 90 °F/32 °C.

HUMIDITY

Orchids require humidity of more than fifty percent. Normal home environment does not offer such humidity levels. Hence, there is need to increase humidity levels around orchids by placing a humidifier. Alternatively, you can place the orchid pots on a tray with many soft black pebbles and cover the pebbles with water to make the atmosphere more humid. However, sufficient ventilation needs to be provided for prohibiting the influx of bacteria. Occasionally, a spray water bottle can be used to provide the necessary humidity to the orchid plants.

WATER

In home environments, orchids are grown in pots filled with bark, stones, tree ferns or some other loosely packed material ensuring that roots are well-aerated and this allows water to drain quickly. Nothing but nothing can kill an orchid as fast as letting it sit in a water-logged pot. Lack of oxygen will cause the roots to suffocate and rot.

Water the orchids, usually about once a week and allow them to dry slightly before watering again. Orchids will be able to withstand periods of forgetfulness but will not be able to bear being overwatered.

AIR CIRCULATION

Air movement is your orchids' best friend. It is vital for the overall health of your orchid. The air movement serves three primary purposes. Gentle wind cools down the plants along with the daily rain showers and high humidity. Air circulation also keeps the temperature more uniform by preventing pockets of cold or hot air in one particular spot. Circulating air prevents disease. Fungus and bacteria germinate and multiply on wet surfaces but with breeze, your plants' leaves will dry more quickly than without. Air circulation can be promoted by not overcrowding the growing area. If the air is getting stagnant, a small fan will help tremendously. Keep in mind that moving air is good as long as it is not too hot or too cold.

FERTILIZERS

Orchids do not require huge amounts of fertilizers. You can use a weak fertilizer solution once a week and can scrape away insect pests gently from the orchid plant. Alternatively, horticultural fine oil or a natural insecticidal soap can be used.

PEST CONTROL

Buying an infested plant is perhaps the most regular way of contracting pests. Isolating the plant for at least two weeks can help restrain diseases. Fulfilling all of the plants' needs is the best action against an impending attack. Plants that are healthy in nature are more resistant to attacks from pests. A clean environment will help reduce any probable pest issue. Faded flowers, dead leaves leaf sheaths, molding, dropped buds and any debris that could give could act as a refuge for pests needs to be removed quickly. This will keep the plant pest free. Most Orchid lovers tend to procure several plants and the growing space gets overcrowded and the plants become a playground for pests and disease allowing it to spread very quickly than those that have enough space to grow.

Ensure that each plant is pest free at least once a week. This way a cannibalization can be detected and treated before it attacks a larger populace. Check all the growing roots and leaves and if pests are found, quarantine the affected ones to prevent further spread. To reduce the risk of developing a pest population that is treatment-resistant, occasionally adopt different methods and by changing the same chemical mix after three or four times. Remain watchful and depending on the spread make applications on a weekly basis to contain the spread.

Before you use any new pest control product it is strictly advisable that you try it on a portion of the plant to ascertain that there are no harm is caused, before extensive use. If a plant shows serious deterioration, a decision must be made if the plant is worth restoring despite continued efforts.

CATTLEYA - QUEEN OF ORCHIDS

Cattleya - an orchid often called the "Queen of orchids" - according to historical sources, was discovered in 1818 by English naturalist William Swainson. This orchid type owes its name to the orchid farmer, owner of one of the largest conservatories, William Cattley. There for the first time this extraordinary plant bloomed in November 1818.

Cattleya in nature occurs in South and Central America, grows in the rainforest and on the sand dunes of the ocean. These orchids are epiphytes, just like Phalaenopsis. They grow not only on tree branches but also on rocks (e.g. Cattleya bowringiana) or on the sand (e.g. Cattleya guttata). Because these orchids are found in different climate zones, they can be divided into three groups according to the temperature they require at night: cold (57-60 °F/14-16 °C), warmth (62-64 °F/17-18 °C) and moderate (64-69 °F/18-21 °C).

Nowadays, you can buy many Cattleya hybrids, which do not cause much trouble in growing. It is important, however, to identify the species used in the crossword, because this will allow you to determine the right temperature of the cultivation and also the appropriate period of rest. This is the primary factor that distinguishes the Cattleya orchid and its hybrids from Phalaenopsis orchids. The resting period is the time from the end of the growth of the new pseudobulb until the time when the flower shoot is formed.

At Cattleyas as new growth matures, the new growth appears at the base of the old pseudobulb, and after a few weeks it produces a flower sheath. After a shorter or longer rest period grows from there a magnificent flower stem with beautiful flowers. Cattleya orchids flowers can reach up to 20-25 cm in diameter, they are usually fragrant but relatively unstable. Flowering lasts from 1 to 10 weeks.

Most Cattleyas are easy to grow. With proper care, these species can be grown anywhere in the world and can be flowered year after year (reliably once, or even twice, a year) which depends on a few basic factors, each of them influenced by the others. They are: 1) light and shade; 2) temperature; 3) humidity; 4) watering; 5) potting and potting medium; 6) repotting; 7) feertilizers. The key of good growing is in achieving a balance of all factors.

Cattleya Queen Sirikhit Diamond Crown

LIGHT

To grow well and bloom, Cattleya need a lot light, though not direct light. The morning sun is very important. The eastern or southern window with slight shading (for example with a translucent curtain) from mid-April to the end of September will be sufficient. Cattleyas orchids with a deep green leaf color mean that they are not getting enough light. Yellow leaf color means excess light.

As much as 95 percent problems in Cattleyas cultivation are caused by too little or too much light.

TEMPERATURE

Cattleya grows best in day temperatures that range from 65° to 85°F (18-29 °C) while night temperatures should be around 55 °F/12 °C (above 60 °F/15 °C). This nightly temperature reduction initiates the formation of flower buds and improves plant growth. Setting of the plant near the window glass will be helpful.

From June to August, the Cattleya can be exposed outside, but be careful, the light has to be filtered. The sun falling directly on the leaf can burn it.

In summer, plants usually tolerate slightly higher temperatures, although overheating of plants exposed to the full south summer sun may end up killing them. In the case of summer temperatures above 95 °F/35 °C on the window sill, shading (e.g. blinds) or moving the orchid to another location is absolutely necessary.

In winter your orchid should not be in contact with frosty air at 32 °F/0 °C or below. Strong frost can lead to the death of the whole plant.

HUMIDITY

Cattleyas like humidity at 45-60%. This can be achieved with a humidifier, or by placing the plant on a tray on which we spread a few-centimeter layer of expanded clay or other porous material, and this is where we put plant pots. When we water the plant, the leaking water leaks through the porous material into the tray. By evaporating gives the plant a higher moisture content. However, make sure the pot are not standing in the water but above it, providing access air to the roots also from the bottom. It is enough to put on the top a metal net or a plastic grille available in garden stores.

WATER

Cattleya orchids water only when the substrate is dry almost to the bottom of the pot. Such drying usually lasts for a week. Besides, small plants can dry faster than large ones. The size of the pot is also important. Large orchids in large pots require less watering, but this does not mean that small orchids need to be planted in large pots, because the substrate dries too long.

If you have doubts as to whether the substrate is sufficiently dry, it is better not to water, just wait a day or two.

In the case of hybrids obtained from plants belonging to different groups, only a careful observation of the development of an orchid allows to determine when the

growth phase and the resting phase begin. Appearing young green roots signal that the plant starts a new period in its life. Then, you should gradually increase watering and fertilizing. The drying time should not be longer than 1-4 days (at rest period not longer than 1-2 weeks).

Rainwater, water from reverse osmosis filter or distilled water is best for watering.

FLOWERING

The growth and flowering process in Cattleya runs in two ways. In the first case, the plant at the end of winter or spring produces a new growth with a flower stem. Then the plant blooms, and as soon as orchids withers, new roots begin to grow from the same pseudobulb. This lasts several weeks, after which the whole process starts from the beginning. In the second case, new growth and roots are formed simultaneously. There is a resting period, during which the sheaths dries taking on the brown color and structure of the parchment. But this dryness is sham only because just after the resting period, beautiful flowers will grow again from there. Therefore, the dried sheath cannot be removed.

POTTING

Potting medium should be characterized by the fact that quickly soaks up water, but also dry rapidly. The plant should not have wet substrate for more than 5-6 hours. If is wet for 2-3 days, it is a signal for transplanting orchid immediately.

This species is usually repotted during the growth of new roots when they reach a length of about 3 cm.

Cattleya feels best in hanging baskets or attached to a piece of branch, bark or cork.

REPOTTING

The substrate should always be ventilated with large air spaces preserved. Normally, pine bark with medium granulation (1-1.5 cm) is used. Transplanting is done every 2 years in spring. It is necessary when the plant grows out of the pot and new growths protrude beyond its edge or when the substrate is decayed. The new pot needs to be large enough to last for 2 or 3 years (1 or 2 new pseudobulbs per year), but it should not be too big because the substrate will not dry fast enough.

Start with a delicate but strong pull of plants from an old pot. Then remove the old substrate from the roots as accurately as possible. Cut out all the dead roots, dead pseudobulbs and place the plant in the new pot so that the oldest pseudobulb was at the edge of the pot. Separating the roots, fill the pot with a new substrate, compressing each portion added gently. The substrate must reach as high as possible to keep the plant in place, with a plug on the surface, about 1.5 cm below the edge of the pot.

To divide, simply remove the plant from the pot and cut the rhizome between the pseudobulbs so that each part has 3-4 fused pseudobulbs. If possible, split the roots. Each part should have at least some roots with active cones of growth. Sometimes it is necessary to cut some roots, but it is usually inevitable and you do not have to be afraid of it. For 2 weeks after transplanting, do not water your orchid. The roots must be healed before the next watering.

PRUNING

Cattleya is not pruned generally.
Old flower stems can be removed after blooming.

FERTILIZING

Use fertilizers for orchids (available in gardening stores and hypermarkets). In summer Cattleyas planted in the bark should be fertilized every second watering, with a half of the recommended dose of fertilizer for orchids. In winter, fertilizing is sufficient every 3-4 weeks.

DENDROBIUM

Dendrobium belongs to the orchid family, which gathers many thousands of species, belonging to different genera, of which the richest species is Dendrobium. Orchids belonging to the dendrobium family, can be found in tropical and subtropical areas both in Asia and Australia.

Dendrobium Nobile Hybrid

Dendrobium orchids are generally referred as epiphytes, which inhabit the boughs of trees and rocks, although there are also terrestrial plants. Their characteristic feature is thickened shoots called pseudobulbs, in which orchids accumulate water and nutrients.

Dendrobium is also characterized by a great diversity of forms and sizes, as well as an impressive array of colors and shapes of flowers. Most of these orchids have quite specific requirements, which are difficult to meet at home. But a few of them can be grown at home, including Dendrobium nobile, Dendrobium phalaenopsis, Dendrobium densiflorum, Dendrobium kingfishum.

LIGHT

Dendrobium orchids require a lot of light throughout the year, but in the summer it is necessary to protect these plants from the burning sun. The light should be as much as the plant will stand without burning the leaves. The amount of light is high enough when the leaves are slightly yellowish. According to the Dendrobium breeders, it tolerates full sunlight outside if it has been acclimated since early spring and has a strong airflow.

TEMPERATURE

Dendrobium is an orchid with moderate heat requirements. Different species of Dendrobium have different requirements in relation to temperature:

- Dendrobium Phalaenopsis does not undergo rest periods, and therefore needs a temperature of 65-71 °F (18-22 °C) throughout the year.
- The remaining Dendrobium species in the autumn and winter months (September to December) must have a rest period, otherwise they will not bloom. During this time orchids should stay in a bright but cool room (night temperature 46-50 °F (8-10 °C), during the day 50-59 °F (10-15 °C). These temperature differences between night and day are optimal for the proper development of flower stalks. With this treatment Dendrobium should release a very large number of flowers in autumn. To get the effect of cooling down, it is best to put orchids in June on the balcony or in the garden in bright partial shade. Orchids should stay outside until mid-October but from the beginning of September watering should be completely stopped. Plants should be protected from rain as well.

Also, placing orchids in the coldest possible place in the flat (for example very close to the glass) and stopping watering for two to three months (from October to the end of December) usually initiates flower buds, but their number is much lower than in case of a cooling outside .

HUMIDITY

Dendrobium needs a lot of air humidity - close to 75% in summer, in winter might fall to 50%.

Humidity should be increased to 45-60% during the development of new pseudobulbs in spring. This can be achieved with a humidifier or by placing the pot on a tray with water and a few centimeters of expanded clay or other porous material.

Also you can systematic spray the plant at the morning using a rainwater or distilled water (a tap water is not recommended).

WATER

Dendrobium orchids grow in a monsoon climate, i.e. with a

high level of precipitation in summer and a period of winter drought. In home cultivation, these conditions need to be restored.

From spring to autumn, orchids should be watered after a slight drying of the substrate. This period can last from 5 to 7 days, depending on the humidity, air movement and light dose. However, in the autumn or winter rest period, after reaching the maturity of the new pseudobulbs, you should completely stop watering and limit yourself to occasional spraying only.

In very dry conditions, when pseudobulbs show visible signs of water shortage, Dendrobium should be lightly watered once every two weeks. Cool and dry rest is very important and should be continue after flowering - until start to growth of new pseudobulbs in the spring.

In active growth, Dendrobium orchids should be watered abundantly, but when new pseudobulbs reach maturity the amount of water should be reduced gradually.

FERTILIZING

Use fertilizers for orchids (from hypermarkets and gardening stores). On the labels of many fertilizers for orchids information is given to fertilize plants every month.

However, you can fertilize them from spring to autumn every week 1/4 or 1/2 of the fertilizer dose recommended on the label (but notice that you need much more water that required for dissolving the fertilizer).

In winter, with limited watering, do not fertilize.

REPOTTING

The substrate should always be well-ventilated with large air spaces. Repotting takes place only in case of spreading the soil (every 2-3 years) or when the plant grows out of the pot. These are the rules for watering with the recommended low mineral content (rainwater, distilled water or reverse osmosis water). However, if you water with tap water (also boiled and stewed), it is necessary to repot every year.

Repotting is done in the spring, as soon as the root activity is noticed. The pot should be as small as possible - in the case of annual repotting (if the plant did not grow rapidly) it may be the same flowerpot.

Dendrobium should never be separated into single pseudobulbs - the minimum division is a group of 3-4 pseudobulbs.

CYMBIDIUM

The Cymbidium orchids are extremely popular in floral decorations. They grow easily in indoor environments and flower in several colors regularly. Cymbidium blooms grow easily and have stunning colors like red and yellow with flowers lasting for many weeks. The flowers are flat and all petals are of similar size.

Cymbidium Mighty Mouse 'Minnie

The cymbidium's area of origin is the foothills of the Himalayas, which means that this kind of orchid is adapted to cold growing conditions. Its flower stems are tall and have 10-25 flowers with a diameter of 6-15 cm. Many of Cymbidium orchids smell nice.

LIGHT

If you grow Cymbidium outside, place the plant in a bright place with filtered light, where in the morning is full sun (under a tree or bush). The afternoon sun is also good. If you grow Cymbidium inside, south, east or west window are the best.

TEMPERATURE

The most important recommendation for the cultivation of cymbidium in the apartment is the need to put them out outdoors (a garden or balcony) from early May until the end of October. These orchids are very fond of night-time temperatures below 57 °F (14 °C). Such low temperatures induce flower stems.

Cymbidiums tolerate temperatures about 33 °F (1 °C). **This orchid will never bloom without keeping low temperature.**

In autumn you should move the plant to a south or east window (it should be as cool as possible).

HUMIDITY

Cymbidiums like humidity at 40-60%, but they are able to tolerate quite dry air in our apartments without much problems. Appropriate humidity can be provided by using a humidifier or by placing the plant on a tray with water and expanded clay. Just make sure that your orchid does not stand in the water, because roots can rot.

You can also fog orchids every morning, but it is important that the leaves are dry before the night. Cymbidiums should not be fogged in winter, because at lower temperatures and with reduced metabolism as well they are more susceptible to rot caused by water remaining in the leaf corners. If you have only a tap water, it is better to give up the fogging entirely because it is very harmful for orchids.

WATER

In spring, summer and autumn Cymbidium should be watered abundantly and often, while in winter, with less sun, watering should be slightly reduced. Except of replanting period, the substrate should be kept constantly moist.

It is also very beneficial to spray the leaves, but only with water of the right quality (rainwater or distilled water). These orchids have long, rather thin leaves, the underside of which is the favorite place for spider mites. To avoid this, once a month, make to your orchid a light shower (with room temperature water). If the spider mites appear again, use a suitable insecticide (one spraying every week).

FERTILIZING

From March to September, fertilize regularly using 1/2 or a full dose of balanced fertilizer for orchids. Then, until February, fertilize once a month with a fertilizer with a lower nitrogen content.

FLOWERING

Cymbidium blooms once a year, its flowers last from 1 to 3 months. Is also very durable as a cut flower.

When all flowers fall down and the flower stem withers, it can be cut low. But take care not to damage pseudobulbs and leaves.

Cymbidium orchids do not release flower stems from the same pseudobulb for the second time. Flower stalks grow only from new pseudobulbs. Old pseudobulbs are no longer active and after 2 years they usually drop leaves It is better not to remove them because they are the storage of water and food for new pseudobulbs.

REPOTTING

When the substrate has decomposed only, because this orchids do not like to disturb the root ball. If orchid requires dividing or repotting, this should be done in spring after the flowering is completed.

Cymbidium produces a huge root system and grow out of pots faster than other orchids. For repotting choose a pot of such size that after placing the plant in the middle there is enough space for a two-year increase at least.

Remove all dead roots and old substrate carefully to not damage alive roots. If you want to divide a plant, each part - in addition to the new growth - must have three or four green pseudobulbs. Cymbidiums are very sensitive to many diseases, so you must sterilize all the tools before using them. All old and leafless pseudobulbs should be cut out when repotting.

Very different substances can be used for substrates, such as Osmond fern roots, fibers, mineral wool or bark, mixed with clay, dry oak leaves, redwood fibers or various combinations of standard horticultural materials. The most important thing is that the substrate should be light, porous and capable of holding moisture. It must drain the water perfectly.

PHALAENOPSIS

Another orchid species, the Phalaenopsis come in rich hues of pink and yellow. They find massive use in wedding bouquets and decorations.

Phalaenopsis

An adult plant has 4 to 8 oval and fleshy leaves with a dark green or marbled color. The leaves are arranged alternately and serve to store nutrients. As new leaves grow, old ones flop, turn yellow and fall off. Flower stems grow between leaves. There may be a several stems and they may branch out, which depends on the variety and plant condition. Flowers can appear throughout the year. Abundance and length of flowering is an individual feature.

In nature Phalaenopsis orchids occur from India, through the south-eastern part of China, Taiwan, the Philippines, Indonesia to Australia. They are epiphytes growing on branches and tree trunks. In stores, we can usually buy them in a transparent, plastic pot, growing in a loose substrate composed of a mixture of bark, expanded clay, pearlite and coconut chips. This substrate's structure allows good air flow and quick drying of the root ball. It can be grown in clay pots, plastic pots, cork pots, in hanging baskets or directly on bark placemats.

Phalaenopsis hybrids offered in stores are easier to adapt to the conditions in our apartments. Their flowers are white, pink, yellow, purple, burgundy, they can also be striped, dotted or spotted. Miniature hybrids of Phalaenopsis with leaves 4-7 cm long and flower stalk 10-20 cm tall are also available in stores.

Phalaenopsis is the easiest orchid to grow. Adapts to the conditions we can provide it and tolerates even significant deviations from the optimal parameters of cultivation. Due to this trouble-free growing, it is often recommended for beginners.

LIGHT

Phalaenopsis likes partial shade. When the light is not enough, the leaves turn dark green instead of slightly yellowish green. It causes elongation of new leaves, which become clearly narrowed in relation to the normal, oval shape. Too much light causes a reddish-burgundy color of the leaves.

Phalaenopsis will feel best in the eastern window, because at the beginning of the day, when the plant receives more light, the temperature is lower. A southern window is possible to grow under one condition: filter the sunlight so that it does not burn the leaves.

On the south or west window, from May to September you need to provide some shade.

TEMPERATURE

The ideal night temperature is 60-64 °F (16-18 °C), and 69-80 °F (21-27 °C) during the day.

In the summer, the plants usually tolerate slightly higher temperatures, but do not put the orchid on the full southern summer sun.

HUMIDITY

Phalaenopsis has a monopodial growth type and has no pseudobulbs as a water storage. That is why it is important to ensure adequate ambient humidity in the range of 50-70%. However, if your orchid is well watered, it can adapt to a lower level of humidity. Phalaenopsis is able to tolerate dry air in our apartments, but will grow and bloom better at higher humidity.

WATER

Water Phalaenopsis only after the substrate is completely dry (indicated by the gray-silver color of the roots). Soft water is recommended for watering: rainwater, distilled water or from reverse osmosis filter with the addition of fertilizer (¼ dose proposed by the manufacturer).

It is best to hydrate by dipping pots with orchids in a container with water at ambient temperature. Time of watering depends on the size of the pot and the type of substrate. It is recommended to water for an hour, not long. The entire substrate should be soaked with water. After removing from the water, the pot should be set aside, preferably on a sieve, so excess water can drain off. Otherwise, the plant will stay in the water for some time, which may cause root rot.

Each orchid should be water separately in a new portion of water. You will avoid transferring diseases between plants. It is worth applying this principle, especially when you often buy new specimens.

FERTILIZING

Phalaenopsis does not go through a resting period, it grows all year long. It is therefore necessary to constantly provide it with the necessary nutrients. The principle is: the smaller the plant, the less fertilizer it needs. The fertilizer dose should be lower that suggested by the manufacturer.

REPOTTING

Repotting is necessary when the substrate in the pot breaks down or the plant grows too much and roots do not fit in the pot. This is an excellent opportunity to check roots condition. Remove roots that are rotten or empty inside.

Phalaenopsis also produces aerial roots which should freely protrude from the pot. When repotting, do not hide aerial roots inside the pot. If the reason for repotting is the decomposition of the substrate, there is no need to change the size of the pot, but when the plant has grown, transplant it into a larger container.

AFTER FLOWERING

There are several ways to deal with flower stems after flowering. The best-known advice is to cut the stalk over the third eye from the bottom. This is not exactly right, because the floral shoot contains many nutrients. It all depends on the condition of the plant.

If the plant is no longer capable of further flowering itself, it will dry the stalk. and then it should be cut off. When condition is good your orchid re-blooms probably on the same stalk - lengthening it - after a short break. We call it a secondary flowering.

It is possible that the plant will dry only the upper part of the stalk and will release the side shoots from the dormant buds. Then it is worth cutting off the stalk leaving about 1 cm of dried part

Sometimes a sick and weak orchid releases a floral shoot for survival. In nature, it would allow the plant to preserve its species. In home cultivation this stalk is only an unnecessary burden for the weakened plant. Is better to cut it off.

ONCIDIUM

Oncidium orchids are slipper shaped. Some of them have a sweet smell and they bloom in vivacious shades like yellow, maroon, white and brown.

Oncidium Divaricatum

The Oncidium family is very large and includes many varieties and over a thousand species. This cultivation instruction concerns Oncidiums most commonly found in florists, which have yellow and mahogany flowers, pear-shaped pseudobulbs and thin leaves.

LIGHT

They grow best in bright, diffused light. The east or west window will be ideal. It may also be a southern window, but you must apply appropriate shading.

TEMPERATURE

In winter, the nighttime temperature should be between 55 and 64 °F (13 and 18 °C), and in summer 60 to 68 °F (16 to 20 °C). However, during the day, the temperature should be between 68 and 86 °F (20 and 30 °C) throughout the year. Lower night temperatures are more important in winter - night temperatures around 59-60 °F (15-16 °C) are optimal.

HUMIDITY

A humidity of 40% or more is required, but it is not a critical factor, although at 60% humidity Oncidiums grow slightly better.

To achieve the right humidity, you can use an air humidifier or a tray with water and expanded clay. You can also fog orchids every morning following the recommendations given in previous chapters.

WATER

Oncidium should be watered just like all epiphytic orchids. Such orchids require watering only after the substrate has dried. Water strongly for 20 minutes to an hour, but rarely - adult plants usually once every 7 to 9 days.

FLOWERING

Depending on the Oncidium variety, a period of flowering may be any season, but usually blooms in autumn and spring. Some hybrids may bloom 2-3 times a year. To initiate flower shoots after the end of growth of the youngest pseudobulb (which has not yet bloomed), the plant must be placed in such a place that the temperature falls below 64 °F (18 °C) at night. Such a cooler place in the apartment can be a window sill. During this time, the amount of water should also be significantly reduced. Water only once every 14-20 days for a period of two months.

As most orchids with a sympodial type of growth, Oncidiums do not bloom from the same pseudobulb for the second time. After blooming, the stem is simply cut (low at the pseudobulb), because the plant does not repeat flowering on the old stalk.

Old pseudobulbs are no longer active and after 2-4 years they drop the leaves. Because they are a storage of water and food for new ones, they should not be cut off.

REPOTTING

From spring to early summer. The flowerpot used should be as small as possible. If yout orchid does not grow rapidly, it can be the same flowerpot. So replanting in this case involves replacing the substrate with new one.

Oncidium planted in bark medium gently remove from the pot. Clean roots from the old substrate, taking care not to break healthy roots. Then cut off all dead, spongy or hollow roots. Healthy roots are white or light beige, firm to the touch, so leave them. The plant is placed in a new pot so the oldest pseudobulb touches its edge, making a place for new ones for the next 1-2 years growth.

Never split Oncidium into individual pseudobulbs - the minimum division is a group of 3-4 fused pseudobulbs.

FERTILIZING

Use fertilizers for orchids available in hypermarkets and gardening stores. If you want to fertilize your orchids every time you water it, every month or every two months the substrate should be rinsed with clean water without fertilizer: first water your orchid normally to dissolve the accumulated salts. After about an hour, the substrate should be rinsed with water equal to twice volume of the pot.

MAINTAIN YOUR ORCHIDS

Phalaenopsis

There is something magical about orchids. Their elegant necks and brilliant petals are suited for a forest habitation but yet they thrive in a home environment with very little upkeep. Like everything else, your orchids need nurturing and care. Maintaining your orchids will ensure that you have exquisite blooms year on year. Repotting orchids periodically prevents their roots from getting overcrowded and hence continue to produce gorgeous blooms.

REPOTTING ORCHIDS

Repotting orchids is to remove orchids from their original pot and thereafter potting them into other pots. Before repotting orchids, make sure you choose the specific type of soil or potting material. The most suitable material is a fibrous, coarse, and a porous substance.

When To Repot Orchids?
Repotting orchids becomes vital in the following conditions.

1. When orchids outgrow and new bulbs and smaller plants coming up do not have space to grow.
2. When the roots begin to rot. You need to clean them and repot them.
3. When the potting medium of orchid starts decaying.
4. When you observe salt buildups on the potting medium.

5. The best times to repot orchids is after they finish blooming and start producing new growth and new roots should be around ½" in length.
6. Never repot a blooming orchid.
7. Do not delay repotting. The flowers in the next season would definitely be less than the earlier years. Sometimes, they may not flower at all.

How To Repot

Choose a pot that is either clay or plastic. You can also create a special orchid pot which has holes on the sides. They allow roots of the orchid plant to grow out. The new pot should be bigger than the original pot. Next, tilt the pot and hold the top of the orchid plant. Now carefully try pulling it out gently and gently tap the pot to loosen the soil. Remove all medium from the roots to loosen and you can use your fingers to separate roots that are tangled together. Cut off dark brown and black roots and trim away thin roots. Keep the healthy roots, which are white or light brown in color. Place the roots well in the new pot and use bark as a growing medium for orchids. They help orchid roots get the required amount of air. Keep the repotted plant in sunlight for the first few days.

Remember!, do not water the orchid for 1 or 2 weeks after repotting, cutted and trimmed roots must recuperate. After this time, water the orchid plant well and it should flow down the bottom of the pot.

TOOLS FOR POTTING PLANTS

You need simple gardening tools for potting orchids. They include a screwdriver for freeing and loosening compost. Pointed blades and sharp knives also prove to be very useful. A piece of hardwood, twelve inches length and thickness of 1½" to 1¾" with one sharpened edge helps in packing the potting the medium firmly.

The ideal pots for repotting orchids depend on what is suitable for the orchid plant. Cattleya, Cymbidiums, and Cypripediums grow best in pots. Certain species like Phalaenopsis grows best in baskets or small pots. Deep pots suit orchids growing in hot and dry climates. Some varieties like Oncidiums and Wanda Coerulea grow best in blocks of wood.

The roots need a lot of free air and so you can tie potting material to the base of the plant to help it grow easily. Select a clear plastic pot to observe and the growth of orchid roots. It is best for the orchids to use as little compost as possible.

If you use a lot of compost, your orchid can drown in the medium. Always place the medium around the roots and do not force to shove it all in. To ensure air circulation, you have to leave it loose. You may also put a layer of gravel at the top of the compost or a layer of rock at the bottom of the pot. This is to ensure extra support.

Your pot should be able to sustain the growth of the orchid for another two to three years. Compost which is well drained suits orchids. If you can water your orchid regularly use open compost. Otherwise, make your compost more water-retentive by mixing bark chippings.

PRUNING

Once the flowers fall off, the time for it to be pruned has arrived so that it can flower again in the next season. Pruning involves removal of dry and wilted stem and leaves and it must be done every year at the second nodule from the base of the stalk. It helps shape the plant and promotes new flower and leaf growth. Orchids usually produce new buds and shoots after pruning and post that they need repotting when they develop new roots. Great care needs to be taken to prune at the right place so as no harm comes on the emerging blooms.

Use of proper pruning tools must be ensured to cut the stem at a distance of one inch from the last flowering node. Ideally, the stem has to be cut when it turns brown. Another pruning method involves cutting the flowering stalk just enough so that it can flower again. In this method cut the stem a quarter of an inch above the nodule so that it can regrow in the next season.

The ideal time for pruning is autumn just before winter which is the flowering season. If you prune in winter all blooming buds will be lost and there will be no flowers. All the dead roots must be removed. Once you prune the orchid, water it once a week and check the roots before watering. If spongy, do not water as excessive water can damage them. Use good orchid fertilizer during the flowering season and the pruned orchids will definitely bloom into beautiful flowers.

SIMPLE TRICKS AND IDEAS

1. Buy healthy plants with good roots. If the roots are not visible do not buy it.
2. Grow only one type of orchid until you the understand the requirements of the specific variety. Pick something that is most suitable to your environment.
3. All growing conditions are not the same. Hence, plan before establishing a water schedule.
4. Do not create a watering schedule without taking into consideration how the plant is potted or mounted and what materials are used. More orchids are killed from overwatering than under watering.
5. Fertilizer must be prudently used. It is easy to burn delicate roots.
6. Orchids don't like high concentrations of salts (fertilizer is a type of salt) because high salt concentrate can destroy orchid roots. Always water before you use fertilizers.
7. Orchid roots need air. Fine medium should be used for orchids that have fine roots and coarser ones for thicker roots.

8. If you are not getting blooms, most likely your orchids need more light. Moderate their exposure to sunlight so that their leaves do not burn.

9. Use an fan for air circulation and this will improve orchid health.

10. Orchids can develop spots in light brown or pink. This is due to fungus or mold. Remove the affected flower and improve air circulation.

11. Deformed flowers is probably because of high temperatures, low humidity levels or virus infections.

12. Cleanliness is vital for prevention of diseases. If infected do not use the same tool from plant to plant.

FREQUENTLY ASKED QUESTIONS

1. Is it essential to have a greenhouse to grow orchids?

No. You can grow orchids in pots as indoor plants or on trees.

2. How long does an orchid bloom remain fresh?

Orchid blooms remain in flowering for different periods. For example: Cattleyas remain in bloom for over a month while Cymbidium and Phalaenopsis remain in bloom for two or three months too. Some orchids bloom many times in a year while some species bloom just once. There are orchid species that bloom all year round.

3. How fragrant are orchids?

Fragrance differs extensively. Some are very while others have a subtle fragrance.

4. What is the ideal temperature for growing orchids?

For most orchids the daytime temperature should be around 75 to 85°F while nighttime temperature should be around 60 to 65°F.

5. When should I use fertilizers on orchids?

Use a good fertilizer every alternate week. However, pre-water orchids before applying fertilizer solution.

6. How often should I water orchids?

Orchids do not require excessive watering. It depends on the weather. Orchids in winter need weekly watering or even fortnightly. In summer, you can water orchids once in four or five days. Never leave orchids in standing water. Ideally, water plants early in the day so that by night, they are dry.

7. Which soil is the best for orchids?

Orchids do not grow in soil and hence there is no best soil. Grow orchids in orchid pot mix or bark mix. They should have good drainage for water to not accumulate at the root because it cuts off air circulation at the roots, which is harmful for growth.

8. When should I repot my orchids?

Repotting of orchids should be done immediately after a bloom. Ideally, you can repot orchids every two years.

9. Why doesn't my orchid bloom?

Orchids may not bloom due to poor light. Proper sunlight can initiate blooming.

10. How to fix the yellow leaves on my orchid?

Old leaves of orchid plants turn yellow and fall off and this is normal. If new leaves of your orchid plant turn yellow, it could be due to lack of nutrition or excess light or low temperatures.

11. What causes the black areas on some parts of my orchid leaves?

The black spots on orchid leaves could be due to bacterial disease or sunburn. Do not expose your orchids to direct and bright sunlight and place orchids in shady areas to keep them receiving little sun.

FROM THE AUTHOR

I would like to ask you for a small favor. Book reviews are very important for other orchid enthusiasts like you. If you have a minute, please leave a comment under my book.
Thank You!

Check Out My Other Books

Bellow you will find my other books that are popular on Kindle.

Phalaenopsis Orchid Care: A How To Guide To Give The Best Life To Your Plant

Orchids Care For Hobbyists: The Advanced Guide For Orchid Enthusiasts

Phalaenopsis Orchids Box Set 2 in 1: Phalaenopsis Orchids Care + Orchids Care For Hobbyists

Orchids Care Bundle 3 in 1: Orchids + Orchids Care For Hobbyists + Phalaenopsis Orchids Care

Health & beauty:

Bath Bombs: Fizzy World Of Bath Bombs, Amazing Recipes To Create Beautiful And Creative Bath Bombs

Natural Hair Care Guide: How To Stop Hair Loss And Accelerate Hair Growth In A Natural Way, Get Strong, Healthy And Shiny Hair Without Chemicals

Essential Oils Guide: The Ultimate Guide To Essential Oils For Weight Loss, Stress Relief, Aromatherapy, Beauty Care, Easy Recipes For Health & Beauty

Essential Oils For Pets: Essential Oils For Dogs: 40 Safe & Effective Therapies And Remedies To Keep Your Dog Healthy From Puppy To Adult

Essential Oils For Cats: Safe & Effective Therapies And Remedies To Keep Your Cat Healthy And Happy

Anti-Aging Skin Care Secrets: Younger Skin Without Scalpel And Botox. Discover How To Rejuvenate Your Skin Quickly And Maintain A Youthful Appearance

Speed reading guide for beginners:

Speed Reading Guide For Beginners: Get Your Fast Reading Skill The Easy Way. Simple Techniques To Increase Your Reading Speed In Less 24 Hours

You can simply search for the titles on the Amazon website to find them. Best regards!